UNDERSTANDING BIBLE TEACHING

Jesus as God

James Philip MA

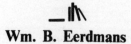

Scripture Union

47 Marylebone Lane, London W1 6AX

Wm. B. Eerdmans

225 Jefferson Avenue, Grand Rapids, Michigan

ISBN 0 85421 709 6 (Scripture Union)
ISBN 0 8028 1765 3 (Wm. B. Eerdmans)

Printed in Great Britain at the Benham Press
by William Clowes & Sons Limited, Colchester and Beccles

General Introduction

There are many commentaries on the Biblical text and there are many systematic studies of Christian doctrine, but these studies are unique in that they comment on selected passages relating to the major teachings of the Bible. The comments are designed to bring out the doctrinal implications rather than to be a detailed verse by verse exposition, but writers have always attempted to work on the basis of sound exegetical principles. They have also aimed to write with a certain devotional warmth, and to demonstrate the contemporary relevance of the teaching.

These studies were originally designed as a daily Bible reading aid and formed part of Scripture Union's Bible Characters and Doctrines series. They can, of course, still be used in this way but experience has shown that they have a much wider use. They have a continued usefulness as a summary and exposition of Biblical teaching arranged thematically, and will serve as a guide to the major passages relating to a particular doctrine.

Writers have normally based their notes on the RSV text but readers will probably find that most modern versions are equally suitable. Many, too, have found them to be an excellent basis for group Bible study. Here the questions and themes for further study and discussion will prove particularly useful—although many individuals will also find them stimulating and refreshing.

ONE

His Deity and Pre-Existence

1 : The Royal Invitation

Matthew 11.20–12.8

The significance of this passage is that it underlines the nature of the controversy between our Lord and the Jewish authorities. It was not His mighty works as such that they objected to, but the claims that were implicit in them. The miracles wrought in Chorazin, Bethsaida and Capernaum were meant to bring about repentance and faith (21–23), the implication being that they were acts of divine power, as was the subsequent pronouncement of woe upon these cities on their refusal to receive His testimony, for who can judge, save God alone?

Our Lord's prayer which follows in v. 25 makes His claim even more explicit, particularly His words in v. 27 which can only be interpreted—as similar teaching was interpreted by the Jews (John 5.16–18)—as the assertion of a unique relationship between Himself and God, that of Sonship. To say that none but the Almighty Father has full knowledge of the mystery of the person and office of the Son, and that none can know the Father except the Son and those to whom the Son reveals Him, is tantamount to His claiming equality with God. It is this that invests the wonderful invitation in vs. 28–30 with such authority and virtue. No mere man could make such an invitation. It echoes the Old Testament appeal, 'Turn to me and be saved, all the ends of the earth', in Isa. 45.22, which is spoken by God Himself.

The same implicit claim lies at the heart of the sabbath controversy in 12.1–8. It is the authoritative re-interpretation

5

of the sabbath law (made in the spirit of the Sermon on the Mount's teaching, 'You have heard that it was said . . . But I say to you', 5.21 f.) that is so impressive and conclusive here. Not only so: our Lord's assertion that 'something greater than the temple is here' (6) makes what can only be called a superlative claim for Himself. The Temple, for the Jews, enshrined the divine presence, and 'something greater' could only mean that in Him the divine presence was incarnate and visible. And if David had the right to 'violate' the law (1 Sam. 21) in what he did when he was hungry, how much more had He, who was the great Lawgiver Himself, the Incarnate Son? The Son of man is Lord of the sabbath because He is the Lord.

2 : The Royal Command

Luke 8.22–39

Two miracles are recorded in these verses, the stilling of the storm on the Sea of Galilee, and the healing of the man with the legion of demons. It is commonplace—as it is almost inevitable—to make these stories apply to the storms of life and its torments, and to draw encouragement from them as we face the hazards and difficulties of human experience. But although this is a legitimate application of the miracles, we must not forget that it is true only because something else— and something greater—is true, namely the fact of the Lordship and Kingship of Christ. The point that all three synoptic writers are intent on making in their Gospels is that Jesus, although truly man, is more than mere man, and they present a series of carefully selected miracles and signs with this in view, before finally recording the critical challenge made by our Lord to the disciples at Caesarea Philippi, 'Who do you say that I am?', and Peter's response, 'You are the Christ, the Son of the living God' (Matt. 16.16). The miracles and signs are meant to elicit such a confession, not only from the disciples, but also from us.

Thus, in the stilling of the storm, Jesus is shown as Lord of nature and the elements, and the disciples 'get the message', saying 'Who then is this, that he commands even wind and water, and they obey him?' (25). No *mere* man could do such a thing; only He who made them could thus control them. In the same way the casting out of the legion of demons shows Jesus as Lord of all dark powers. (We must not make the mistake of equating demon-possession with psychiatric disorder, for the two are not the same. In fact, the Gospel writers sometimes make a clear distinction between the two even when the presenting symptoms are the same in both cases, as a comparison of Matt. 9.32 f. with Mark 7.32 and Matt. 15.30 will show). This claim to Lordship and Deity is implicit in Jesus' words to the healed man, and in his response. He is commanded to return home and declare how much *God* has done for him; he immediately proclaimed how much *Jesus* had done for him. Is not the implication here unavoidable?

3 : The Light of the World

John 8.12–24

The sublime words in v. 12 form a companion with John 7.37 f., and both refer to the ritual performed at the Feast of Tabernacles, the one to the pouring of water from the Pool of Siloam on the altar by the priests, symbolizing God's provision of water in the wilderness, the other to the illumination of the Temple courts, symbolizing His guidance by the pillar of cloud and fire. Jesus claims to be the fulfilment of both. The claim in v. 12 is therefore a Messianic claim (cf. Isa. 42.6; 49.6), and the Pharisees recognize it as such and dispute it. The 'I am' would have deep significance for them, being the Divine Name of the Old Testament (cf. Exod. 3.14). The discussion that follows shows their need of light. It is His authority that they question and challenge in v. 13. They may be quoting Jesus' own words in 5.31, 'If I bear witness to myself, my testimony is not true.' If so, this betrays a shallow understanding of His meaning, and a lack of appreciation of who He is. There is no contradiction. Indeed, He goes on to say that His authority and the truth of His witness reside in the fact that He knows where He has come from and where He is going—a clear reference to His eternal Sonship. On this ground He claims the right to be heard.

Something important emerges here: on the one hand, there is, ultimately, no mere rational proof of our Lord's authority; and on the other, once a man perceives His deity, there is no further question of the authority of His words. One does not prove Christ; one believes in Him. The Pharisees were blind to His identity, knowing Him only 'after the flesh.' This is borne out in vs. 16 ff. If they had a mind to believe, there was sufficient 'evidence' on the rational level to satisfy them law-wise (17), for the Father also bore witness to Him (cf. 5.31 ff.), and this fulfils the rabbinic requirement (17 f.). They ask, 'Where is your Father?', not 'Who?' speaking with contempt, thinking His father to be Joseph, the carpenter. But to see no more in Jesus than a human, historical figure, is not to see Him at all. The gulf between them was complete. They understood neither His person nor His work. This was their condemnation and their eternal loss.

4 : The Royal Claim

John 8.25–47

The question 'Who are you?' addressed to Jesus in v. 25 is given an unmistakable answer, for those with ears to hear, in the debate between our Lord and the Jews which occupies the remainder of this chapter. There is only one ground on which the claims implicit in His teaching can be regarded as either credible or free from the charge of blasphemy, namely that of His deity. Jesus' deliberate use of the words 'I am' in v. 28 (there is no 'he' in the original), His claim that continuing in His word means knowing the truth that makes men free (31 f.), and that He can set men truly free (36), His assertion that true children of God will necessarily love Him, the Son, all alike imply and assume His Godhead. Indeed, they do so in such a way that the only real alternative to falling down and worshipping Him was to brand Him as a blasphemer and put Him to death. He did not leave it open either to His hearers or to us to think of Him as only a great religious teacher. It must be the one or the other. There is no intermediate position.

This 'either-or', and the cruciality of His deity for true faith are borne out by a distinction John makes in the two Greek constructions for 'believed' he employs in vs. 30 and 31. From the first we can deduce a faith that involves personal reliance, trust and commitment; from the second, however, in v. 31, we can assume a faith that was merely nominal and superficial, akin to that of certain disciples in 2.23, where we are told that Jesus was not prepared to commit Himself to them. Jesus' words to the Jews that believed in this way have therefore the effect of sifting them, and exposing the fatal lack in their attitude to Him. Hence their immediate reaction in v. 33, objecting to the suggestion that they needed to be made free, and their increasing resistance to His radical probing of their basic attitudes (37, 39). The more He says, the more they reveal their fundamental lack of understanding of the things of God, a blindness due to their unwillingness to receive His testimony concerning Himself (43); until belief in Him that refuses to acknowledge His deity is finally exposed as being of the devil (44). So central is the doctrine of the deity of Christ for true, saving faith.

5 : The Eternal Christ

John 8.48–59

The accusation of demon-possession levelled against Jesus in these verses marks a climax in the conflict between Jesus and His critics, and exposes the depth of their unbelief and their inability to receive His testimony concerning Himself. One thing is clear, not only from these verses, but also from those which precede them: the Jews were in no doubt as to the kind of claim Jesus was making for Himself. They knew He was claiming Messiahship and Deity; and since such a claim to Deity was unthinkable, the only possible alternative must be that He had a devil. Only one who was either devil-possessed or the Messiah could dare to speak as Jesus does in v. 51. This is what lies behind the contemptuous question they ask in v. 53, 'Are you greater than our father Abraham?' To this Jesus answers two things: firstly, that Abraham 'rejoiced that he was to see my day; he saw it and was glad.' Jesus means and implies that Abraham's faith looked forward to His own coming, and indeed rested upon that coming; and by implication He indicates that the faith of all the old dispensation was faith in the promise of His coming. Secondly, He uttered perhaps the most profound of all His statements, 'Before Abraham was, I am.' These words not only serve to reinforce the earlier claim in v. 56, making even more explicit His pre-existence, but also in the use of the sacred 'I am' emphasize His eternal pre-existence and His essential Deity. This assumption of the divine Name of the Old Testament could lead only to worship and adoration, on the part of those who believed in Him, and the assumption of blasphemy, on the part of those who did not. It was on this ground that they took up stones to throw at Him (59).

6 : Jesus—Word of God Incarnate

John 1.1–5; 20.19–29

The association of ideas in these two passages, one from the prologue of John's Gospel, the other from the Resurrection narratives, is considerable, and serves to underline John's essential message. For one thing, in what is perhaps the most sublime passage in the New Testament, the apostle identifies the One of whom he is to write and speak as being the eternal Word by whom all things were made. This is He, the light and life of men, who was made flesh (1.14), and entered into death and passed through it to victory 'for us men and for our salvation.' It is when we view the death of Christ in this light that we see, as Peter made plain on the day of Pentecost (Acts 2.24), that death could not hold Him, but had to concede the victory to Him. It was the eternal Son who entered into death: it could not but be abolished, bringing to birth a gospel of life and immortality. The darkness could not overcome the light that had invaded it (1.5).

10

This is the significance of the risen Christ's words to the disciples in **20**.19, 21, 'Peace be with you'. There was now nothing left, death being vanquished, to prevent or disturb their peace. John may have had the original creation story in mind when writing these words, for, as in the beginning, the sabbath rest and peace of God were disturbed by the entrance of sin, so here peace is restored by the Creator-Redeemer God. Also, on the first day of creation God said, 'Let there be light', and there was light; and now, on the first day of the week—the first day of the new creation, so to speak— light came once again to the disciples: 'Then the disciples were glad when they saw the Lord' (**20**.20).

In this context, the episode of Thomas's doubt is seen to be without excuse. If Christ be the eternal Son who has become incarnate and passed through death, His risen, victorious Presence really commands belief and trust. And Thomas, when he realizes the truth of the situation, emerges from doubt into true faith, confessing Christ as his Lord and his God. This is the logical, inevitable conclusion to which John's Gospel is designed to lead us. In the light of this fact how impossible becomes the translation of **1**.1 ('The Word was a god') advanced by the Jehovah's Witnesses! It does justice neither to the grammar of the Greek (see the larger commentaries for the technicalities), nor to the place of the statement in a Gospel which leads up to the great confession of Thomas.

7 : The Mighty Indwelling

Colossians 1.9–23

Paul's prayer in vs. 9–12a that the Colossians would lead a life worthy of the Lord follows the usual apostolic pattern of basing exhortations to holiness and fruitfulness on the doctrines of the faith. Ethical imperatives rest on the indicatives of grace which are their inspiration and dynamic. Here, these indicatives concern the person and work of Christ. Every phrase in the sustained theological treatment of this theme is charged with deep significance. Christ is the image of the invisible God (15). He both represents and manifests

11

the Father, not merely in His pre-incarnate existence as the second Person of the Trinity, but also in His existence now as the glorified Lord in heaven. He is also the first-born of all creation. This does not mean that He was the first of the created beings. He was not created at all, as v. 17 makes clear. The NEB and J. B. Phillips both capture the real sense when they say 'His is the primacy over all created things' (NEB) and 'He existed before creation began' (J. B. Phillips). Priority and sovereignty over all creation is what is meant, and this is expanded in vs. 16 and 17. 'He is both the first principle and the upholding principle of the whole scheme of creation' (J. B. Phillips).

The particular aspect of Christ's redeeming work that Paul emphasizes here is reconciliation. Two points in particular must be underlined. First of all, Paul says that this reconciling Christ is the great Creator Himself. The work of reconciliation is so vast and infinite that only One who was God could accomplish it. No one who was less could ever have done what Jesus did. For reconciliation is the putting away by God of God's own condemnation of the world and its sin, and its message is that the awful barrier between man and God has been removed once for all by an awful demonstration of divine love, by God Himself, in the Person of His Son. Secondly, Paul places this message of man's reconciliation in a larger, vaster context—the reconciliation of 'all things, whether on earth or in heaven' (20). It is this universal cosmic reconciliation in which man shares, and of which his is a part, albeit the significant and decisive part. Well might Paul exclaim that such a Christ is pre-eminent and that 'in Him all the fullness of God was pleased to dwell'!

8 : God's Last Word to Men

Hebrews 1.1–2.4

The theme of Hebrews is the excellency of Christ, and His superiority to everything in Judaism. The opening statement (1 f.) is one of the most majestic utterances in all Scripture, sounding out like the movement of a great symphony and,

12

symphony-wise, announcing the principal subject matter of all that follows. The writer contrasts how God spoke 'of old' —in shadows, in illustrations, in the law, in history, through the prophets—with how He has spoken 'in these last days' in Christ. In none of the former was His full revelation given, and something still remained to be said. Christ is God's last word to man, for in Him He answers all the need of humanity.

This Son in whom God has spoken is described in language that stresses His unique, solitary excellence. He is 'heir of all things' (1.2), that is, everything in creation exists for Him, a stupendous claim forcing us to conclude that He could not have been a mere created being, but One who is eternal (and consequently immeasurably superior to angels, who are created beings). Thus we come to the thought of His involvement in creation itself—'through whom also he created the world'. 'Before Abraham was, I am,' Christ once said, and He could have said as truly, 'Before creation was, I am.' The force of the description of Christ in v. 3a lies in the significance it gives to what follows in v. 3b, as if to say, 'It took such an One as this eternal, all-glorious One, who is God the Son, to deal with sin.' It is this mighty work, including within its compass the resurrection and ascension, that constitutes God's word to men. It is a word of pardon and salvation that He speaks in Christ.

The rest of the chapter establishes the superiority of Christ, and the revelation given in Him, over the angels. The old Arian doctrine of the 4th century and the teaching of modern Jehovah's Witnesses and Christadelphians virtually reduces the pre-incarnate Christ to a kind of super-angel. For our writer, however, they are servants, He is the Son (4–6); they are subjects, He is the King who reigns over them (7–9); they are creatures, He is Creator (10-14). And by virtue of His victory He has been elevated to His superlative position at the right hand of God, and towers over the created order as its King and Head. Hence the warning in 2.1–4. If the message declared by angels was worthy of serious attention, how much more the message of the King of angels, in whom such a great salvation is proclaimed to men?

13

Questions and themes for study and discussion on Studies 1-8

1. Is it the greatness of man's need, or the authority in the invitation in Matt. 11.28, that constrains him to come to Christ?

2. On the evidence given in Luke 8.22-39 what do *we* think of Christ?

3. How does Paul's statement in 2 Cor. 5.16 help us to understand the Jews' attitude in John 8.12-24?

4. What are the marks of true faith, according to the teaching of John 8.25-47?

5. Jesus said Abraham saw His day (John 8.56), yet the Jews in reply spoke of His seeing Abraham. Why did they turn the statement round? Did they really understand what He meant?

6. How does John show (John 20.19-29) that the darkness (1.5) has not overcome the light?

7. How does Paul's teaching in Col. 1.9-23 compare with John's in the prologue to his Gospel?

8. How does the teaching of Heb. 1 compare with that of Paul and John?

9. Is there really any value in saying we accept the authority of the Bible if we evade its teaching as to the deity of Jesus, as Jehovah's Witnesses and others do?

TWO

His Incarnation and Virgin Birth

9 : Immanuel—God with Us

Isaiah 7.1–17

The reference to Immanuel in this prophecy needs to be understood in its historical context, which is unfolded in 2 Kings 16.1–9. Syria and Israel have entered into a coalition against Judah, and Isaiah exhorts Ahaz to trust in the Lord, and to appeal for help to Assyria. Seeing, however, that the king was not disposed to take his advice, he appealed to him to seek a sign from the Lord. But Ahaz, knowing that any sign from God must simply confirm Isaiah's word to him, refuses to do so, whereupon Isaiah announces that God would give him a sign. On one interpretation this was a sign of judgement instead of grace. The sign would be simple enough to interpret but for the name Immanuel involved in it. A child born of a virgin was to be the divine sign, and by the time he was come to years of discretion he would be eating curds and honey, which, on this interpretation, was the food of privation and desolation, of a people whose land, depopulated by the enemy, had been turned into pasture. In a matter of a few years, Syria and Ephraim were to be laid waste and Judah made desolate. But why should the wonderful name Immanuel, God with us, be associated with judgement, when it is so inseparably associated with the promised Messiah? The link is this: the child would become an innocent Sufferer, a Man of sorrows. There is a marvellously mysterious interweaving of events here to produce the picture of a suffering Servant. G. Adam Smith refers to Ahaz

15

as the Judas of the Old Testament, who sells the Messiah by wilfully seeking to bring about the kingdom in his own sinful way. The name Immanuel, God with us, must surely have pointed the true way to Ahaz. Trust in Him, cried Isaiah, not in Assyria. But Ahaz was intent on going his own way, and as such stands as the symbol of a people of God whose continued faithlessness caused the Christ to be born into a subject race. Here is the beginning of the rejection of the Messiah by a people who knew not the time of their visitation. The sign may well have found its immediate fulfilment in one whose mother was still a virgin when the prophecy was given, but it reaches out beyond him to a greater than he. And the instinct of the New Testament Church was right when it saw in these words a Messianic hope and regarded them as fulfilled in the birth of Christ.

10 : The Virgin Birth of Christ

Matthew 1.18–25

The essential point that Matthew makes here is that there was something uniquely special and different about the birth of Jesus. What is the mystery of the virgin birth meant to teach us? It is not simply that it was necessary in order to ensure that Jesus would be sinless, not partaking of the heritage and taint of sin through Joseph—for would not the taint have been inherited equally through Mary? Rather, the mystery and the miracle lie in this, that in the divine provision of salvation man, as man, is completely set aside. 'The male, as the specific agent of human action and history, with his responsibility for directing the human species, must now retire into the background, as the powerless figure of Joseph' (Barth). It is this setting aside of man as such that is the real heart of the biblical testimony, and it tells us that that part in us that wants to do, and indeed insists on doing, something active for our own salvation is resolutely and firmly set aside by God. Salvation is of God, and all of grace.

Furthermore, the doctrine declares unequivocally that here, in Jesus Christ, God is beginning a new thing. Matthew has already hinted at this in the phrase 'the book of the genealogy of Jesus Christ' (1.1), which echoes similar phrases in Gen. 2.4 and 5.1 about the 'generations of Adam', as if to suggest that as Genesis tells the story of the tragic fall of the first Adam, so now he is to tell the story of the second Adam which is the divine answer to man's need. This becomes even more explicit in the statement that Mary was found to be with child of the Holy Spirit, for this perhaps echoes Gen. 1.2, where 'the Spirit of God was moving over the face of the waters'. Here, then, was an act of new creation. The old humanity, in spite of its glory and promise, had come to grief, and now the new humanity, signifying a complete break with the old, and a new beginning, was being ushered in. And as by its sin the old humanity had been cut off from God, so now the new order was to be characterized by a reversal of this tragedy. God had come to men once more—Emmanuel, God with us.

11 : The Divine Visitation

Luke 1.26–45

Luke's account of the virgin birth of Christ takes us behind what Matthew tells us to the manner in which our Lord's birth came about. The passage contains three lessons of enormous significance. First is the fact of the divine visitation. The angel Gabriel comes to Mary to announce the Saviour's birth. It is a moment of destiny in which the sovereign Lord of the universe approaches His creature, bestowing on her the unique privilege of becoming the mother of the Saviour of the world. All Old Testament history is summed up in this confrontation—through the primal work of creation, the experiences of Abraham, the wilderness wanderings, Judah's and Israel's backslidings, and the turmoil of the Captivity, God had His eyes steadily fixed on this encounter; and all His dealings with His people were designed to lead to this crucial moment. As Paul says, the time had fully come (Gal. 4.4). Mary's question 'How?' in v. 34 underlines the mystery we also feel here, and the angel's answer tells us as much as

17

we shall ever understand. The birth was to be a divine visitation, and the Spirit of God was to overshadow her, as that Spirit had once brooded upon the face of the deep in the beginning of creation, to create in her this unique Life that was to be the life of men.

The second lesson lies in Mary's response to the message of the angel. Two things are said about this. On the one hand, Elizabeth speaks of Mary's confidence that the promise given her would be fulfilled (45). Her response to the angelic annunciation was one of true faith. But, on the other, faith for her meant submitting to the word of the Lord, abandoning herself to it and to its power in her life (38). And her blessedness (45) consisted in that, having been chosen for this special service, and having received an amazing promise, she rose unreservedly to the summons of God in obedience and submission.

Finally, the angel's words in v. 35 beautifully illustrate what has been called 'the virgin birth of faith in the soul'. What the angel said would happen to Mary also happens to men through the preaching of the Word. This is how men are born of the Spirit; and the newness of life they receive is the coming of the Christ to dwell in their hearts.

12 : God Manifest in the Flesh

John 1.6–18

The central affirmation that John makes concerning the Incarnation is that it is the eternal Word, by whom the worlds were made, that became flesh in the Babe of Bethlehem, and dwelt among us. It will be enough, in studying this passage, to try to understand something of the meaning of this astounding statement.

What does John mean to convey by saying that the Word became flesh? He does not, and cannot, mean that He ceased to be what He was before, and became something else, as the more extreme 'Kenosis' theologians maintained. He did not cease to be God, although He became man. To say that He came in disguise, incognito, conveys something of the mystery,

18

The Godhead of the Son

n 1.1–4; 4.1–6

opening words of John's Epistle deal with the same
ct as the Prologue to his Gospel, namely the eternal
xistence and historical manifestation of the Son of God.
apostle's assertion is that the Eternal, the Invisible, the
gible, has been manifested in a historical Incarnation
ch a way that men could hear, see and handle it. The
rlying presupposition of all his teaching is the breaking
om beyond of the Power behind all power, a super-
al visitation that conditions all existence, for weal or
In this categorical statement, John effectively demolishes
ontentions of the heretics of his day, the false prophets
.1. It is the Eternal Son, none other, who has been
nate in history, the Eternal God who has entered time
e person of Jesus. He who is from the beginning is one
the same as He whom the apostles heard, saw and
led. It is impossible, John implies, to distinguish as the
ics did, between the historical Jesus and the eternal
t, for the Eternal Son *is* Jesus, and He came down
seen of men. It is impossible, therefore, for them to say
the Incarnation was only a seeming one, and that the
st' came upon Jesus only at His baptism and left Him
re He died on the cross. This heresy is known as
tism (from the Greek *dokein* 'to seem to be'). Any
eption of our Lord's person which does not take His
anity seriously may be broadly defined as 'docetic'. For
an to deny that Jesus Christ is come in the flesh, means
he is not of God, but of the devil (4.3).

ch is the apostolic proclamation (1.3); and the grand aim
s in view is that through this incomparable message men
be restored to fellowship—with God and with His Son
Christ and, through them, with all the company of the
ful—and brought into fullness of joy (1.4). In thus
ning up the essence of the meaning of the gospel, John
s the absolute cruciality of the Incarnation, and pro-
s a standard or norm by which to assess the worth of
man's message. 'Put them to this test,' he says. 'If they
ot confess the Godhead of the Son, they are not of God.'
as simple as that. If Jesus is not God manifest in the

(although in another sense this is just as misleading). Behind
the disguise there is the Person of God the Son. He it is who
is come in the flesh (1 John 4.2), not another, and when Paul
speaks of His emptying Himself (Phil. **2.**7), that self-emptying
must be understood as the laying aside of the *mode* of divine
existence which He enjoyed with the Father, not the laying
aside of what He was, and is. He became a servant but there
was never a moment, not even in the manger, when He
ceased to be God. The idea of a disguise, however, is misleading in that, for us, a disguise is something we dispense
with when it is no longer needed. But Jesus Christ does not
lay aside His human 'disguise'. He has become man for ever.
'Manhood taken by the Son' was not a temporary expedient,
but something done once for all and for ever. It is the
permanent hallowing and sanctifying of humanity.

On the other hand, the word 'flesh' must be taken with real
seriousness. God the Son really became man. The humanity
of Christ was, and is, real and complete. He was, and is, fully
and permanently man. This is mystery indeed, but the mystery
must be accepted. Jesus is divine and Jesus is human, both
God and man. He has two natures, the divine and the human,
united in one Person, the God-man. The Word is not made
flesh by changing one nature into another, or by laying aside
one nature and taking up another, but by the Godhead taking
manhood. To grasp this fact is to be delivered from much
heretical thinking, both ancient and modern. The Incarnation
is the mystery of God manifest in the flesh.

13 : The Mystery of Godliness

1 Timothy 3.14–4.6

This passage contains one of the richest expressions of
Christian truth in existence (3.16). Many scholars think it is a
quotation from an ancient credal hymn in use in the early
Church. The form of the sixfold statement suggests a hymnal
construction, falling into two parts or 'verses', the first
describing the life of the incarnate Son of God on earth, the
second the life of the glorified Lord in heaven. (Incidentally,

'the mystery of our religion' (RSV) means 'the open secret of our piety', and refers to Christ Himself (cf. Eph. 3.4). The passage speaks of the Incarnation but the RSV omits the word 'God' on textual grounds.)

Paul's words 'He was manifested in the flesh' are a direct equivalent of John 1.1–14. The eternal Word became man, coming from beyond time into time for our sakes. This clearly implies Christ's pre-existence before Bethlehem, but also proclaims that the human Jesus was the divine, eternal Son. Christ remained God the Son when He became man. Some take 'vindicated in the Spirit' to refer to the whole of Christ's earthly life and work being borne testimony to by the Spirit; others, to the resurrection, by which he was 'designated Son of God in power' (Rom. 1.4); others, as covering the whole of biblical revelation, including the testimony of the Spirit to Him in Old Testament days—i.e. in prophecy, in His earthly life, and finally in His resurrection. 'Seen of angels' is a striking concept, suggesting the wonder and awe with which the angels of God viewed the unfolding mystery of the Incarnation.

'Preached among the nations' sums up the whole of the Acts, and indeed all Church history. It was for this that the divine promise in Christ's life, death and resurrection was fulfilled, that there might be a gospel to preach to all men. The grandeur of Paul's thought here thrills the heart. While the angelic world was admiring on high the matchless grace of God, the world of men below was hearing and responding to the glad sound of the gospel. This is the force of 'believed on in the world'. Faith comes by hearing, and the power of the self-manifestation of God is such that it bends the wills and reconciles the hearts of men to Himself. 'Taken up in glory' speaks of Christ's 'official' appointment to the place of power and authority as Victor over sin and death and hell. It is His coronation, on the basis of which He exercises His kingly rule and ministers the benefits of His earthly mediatorial work to men. Great, indeed, is the mystery of our religion!

14 : Born to Die

Hebrews 2.5–18

These verses unfold the meaning and purpo Incarnation. The writer's concern is to reco Jesus is immeasurably superior to the ang apparently incongruous fact of His being in shame and ignomiy. The argument fro it is a prediction of 'the world to come', a man, though reduced for a period of time b the angels, is yet destined to occupy the hig God's creatures, and that this transformatior by our Lord's becoming man. Thus, He is while lower than the angels (v. 9), He beco (v. 11), He partakes of our nature (v. 14), His brethren in every respect (v. 17). It is man that qualifies Him for this task, but by becoming man that He fulfils it. Rather, in order to die (for God is deathless and so it is by His death that He accomplishes n and secures to him his ultimate destiny in th

The writer makes three statements abou Christ, each being represented as fulfilling His having become man. The first, in v. 9 having tasted death for everyone. Death he death as we know it, but death as the wa Jesus drank that cup to its bitter dregs, that have to do so. The second statement, in v. through death Christ destroyed him who ha death, that is, the devil. The death He died ground on which He grappled with and con powers that lie behind the woes of man, c not in the sense of putting them out of e robbing them of their power over man. The v. 17, speaks of Christ making expiation for people. The word in the Greek is better tran tion', and speaks of the controversy that between God and man, and the turning awa anger by the atoning blood of the Mediato the Son of God became incarnate.

flesh, there is no gospel, no true atonement, and no forgiveness of sins.

16 : Christ is Victor

Revelation 12

The book of Revelation divides naturally into two parts, chs. 1-11 and 12-22. In the first, the main theme is the conflict between the Church and the world, in the second, we are shown that that conflict is the outward manifestation of the war between Christ and the powers of darkness. The world and the hearts of men are the battleground of spiritual forces striving for the victory. Here we have the picture of a dragon standing before a woman about to give birth to a child, ready to destroy it. The child is born, and is caught up to God and His throne. The woman flees to the wilderness, where God has prepared for her food and shelter (1-6). Then (7-12) we see war in heaven, and the dragon is cast from heaven to earth. The dragon immediately persecutes the woman (13-17) and she experiences the care and protection of God.

The child in this symbolic picture is Christ, and the testimony of John's words is that the fundamental battle between good and evil in the universe centres upon Him. The woman symbolizes the one people of God throughout the ages, the Israel of God from whom the promised Messiah comes. This, therefore, is a pictorial representation of the Incarnation, a telescopic picture of the history of the Old Testament revelation culminating in the fulfilment of the promise made in the Garden of Eden (Gen. 3.15). Christ is the promised Seed, born to do battle with the dragon, that old serpent the devil. But Christ's work of redemption is not accomplished through the Incarnation alone: He is 'caught up to God and to His throne' (5), a clear reference to His ascension, which completed the 'movement' begun by His coming down to earth for our sakes. The consequences of this are described in vs. 7-12: Satan as accuser of the brethren is cast out, and is no longer able to bring any charge against God's elect (Rom. 8.33). It is this that constitutes victory for the people of God, and is the ultimate purpose of the Incarnation, a purpose which not all Satan's pressures and attacks can avail to frustrate (13–17). They may be 'killed all the day long' as the chapter indicates, but in all these things they will be 'more than conquerors through him who loved us' (Rom. 8.36 f.).

Questions and themes for study and discussion on Studies 9-16

1. How does the 'child' in Isa. 7 illustrate the Pauline statement that 'God chose what is weak in the world to shame the strong'?
2. What is Matthew's purpose in linking the birth of Jesus with the Old Testament prophecies?
3. What does Luke's account of the Annunciation have to tell us about the nature and reward of faith?
4. Could Christ fully make God known to men if He were not wholly divine as well as truly human?
5. What does 1 Tim. 3.16 reveal about the early Church's grasp of Christ's 'finished work'?
6. What does Heb. 2.5–18 tell us about the relation between the Incarnation and the Atonement?
7. Why is the Deity of Christ (1 John 1.1–4) so essential for the very existence of the gospel?
8. What does Rev. 12 tell us about the nature of Christ's victory on the cross?

THREE

His Character

17 : 'He Suffered being Tempted'
Luke 4.1–15

The story of our Lord's temptation is best understood in the context of His purpose in coming into the world to be our Saviour. He is presented in the Gospel record as the second Adam, and it is this fact that gives significance to the temptations He endured, for they follow the general pattern of the temptations that came to the first Adam in the Garden of Eden. Adam and Eve were tempted to eat unlawfully (Gen. 3.1, 5); so was Christ (3). Adam and Eve were promised godlike power: 'You will be like God, knowing good and evil' (Gen. 3.5); so was Christ: 'If you, then, will worship me, it shall all be yours' (7). Adam and Eve were tempted in relation to God's word, through Satan's lying assurance, 'You will not die'; so was Christ, through the subtle misapplication of the promise of God, 'He will give His angels charge of you'. The decisive difference between the two encounters is that whereas Adam and Eve fell, Christ stood firm and unmovable. Viewed in this light, Christ's temptation represents the beginning of the counter-offensive against the kingdom of darkness that was to lead to final victory in the triumph of the cross.

It is the obedience of Christ to the will of God, and His holy determination to live in submission to His word that invests His character with incalculable worth and makes His life of such infinite value when offered in atonement for the sins of the world. In the Old Testament economy, the sacrificial lamb had to be without blemish and without spot. Christ

25

is the truth of all the sacrifices, and He offered Himself without blemish to God for our sins.

Luke tells us that Jesus was 'full of the Holy Spirit' as He came to the wilderness from His baptism; but after His encounter with Satan, He returned to Galilee 'in the power of the Spirit'. The difference in phraseology is significant. As G. Campbell Morgan puts it, 'Fullness of the Spirit becomes the power of the Spirit through processes of testing. . . . The power of the Spirit is never realized save through some wilderness of personal conflict with the foe. From such experience, entered upon in the fullness of the Spirit, men go out either broken and incapable of service, or with the tread and force of conscious power.'

18 : The Challenge of Discipleship

Mark 10.17–22, 35–45

The story of Christ and the rich young ruler teaches us many lessons about the nature of discipleship. First, to his question about eternal life, Jesus' reply 'Why do you call me good?' has a deeper significance than is at first apparent. Rightly understood it is an assertion of His Deity. In effect He was saying, 'Do you realize that it is God the Son you are speaking to? Either I am God, or I am not good, for only God is good.' If only he had seen that it was God, the Fount of life, who was speaking to him! 'I am eternal life, man, can't you see? Follow Me—that is the answer to your need.' Such was the challenge that met the ruler. But he was blind to the implications of the encounter, and when Jesus uncovered the secret idol in his life, he was shattered by the inexorable demand made upon him, in a way he would not have been if he had recognized his divine Challenger to be the Source and Giver of life itself. So, having come to the very gates of heaven, he went away sorrowful. And Jesus let him go. He is not prepared to lower the price of discipleship. With Him it must be all or nothing. The 'halfway house' has no place in His scheme of things.

The radical nature of discipleship thus underlined is further emphasized in vs. 35–45, as indeed is the true nature of goodness. When Jesus summoned the ruler to a discipleship with a cross at its heart, He was calling him to adopt His own pattern of life. 'Goodness', for Jesus, meant a life of service and sacrificial giving; it meant drinking a cup, and being baptized with a baptism, of suffering (38). The disciples were then as far out in their thinking about true goodness as the young ruler was, as the request made by James and John in vs. 35–37 shows, but our Lord's insistence on the principle of 'dying to live' (42–44) was ultimately to bear fruit in their lives, as we see in Acts. It is one of the hardest lessons in spiritual life to learn that in a fallen world real goodness can be expressed only in terms of suffering love.

Our subject is the Person of Christ. This study demonstrates that discipleship means commitment to Christ and takes His own character and sacrificial style of life as its pattern. So the Christian disciple needs to 'Consider Him!'

19 : The Supremacy of Love

1 Corinthians 13

The context of this wonderful chapter is Paul's discussion of the gifts of the Spirit which, he says, are distributed among the members of the Church, and by definition are not, and cannot be, the portion of all alike. By contrast, he now speaks of something within the reach of the humblest and most ordinary believer. The central reality in Christian experience is not the exercise of spiritual gifts, but the practice of Christian love.

The chapter divides naturally into three sections. In the first (1–3), love is contrasted with other religious actions and attitudes, and Paul takes up the spiritual gifts mentioned in the previous chapter—tongues, prophecy, discernment, knowledge, faith, benevolence ('helps', AV)—and indicates that these may flourish in believers' lives without love. When they do, life is empty; and by themselves they are not necessarily an evidence of a right relationship with God.

In the second section (4–7), love—this quality whose

27

absence is so deadly and fatal to the Christian life—is described in both positive and negative terms. What love is, is shown by what love does. Actions speak louder than words. The personification of love that Paul makes in these verses is significant, and it is not difficult for us to see that he is thinking of Jesus. It is for this reason we have included this chapter in this series of studies. Jesus Christ is the embodiment of love, and these qualities are fulfilled supremely and only in Him. And when He lives in our hearts by His Spirit, it is the loving Jesus that should be revealed in our actions. Love is an outgoing quality, self-forgetful and self-effacing, far removed from the self-regard and self-expression that sometimes characterize the exercise of spiritual gifts.

In the final section (8–13) love is represented as enduring and victorious, in contrast to even the best of gifts. These latter are all at best but partial revelations of the God who is love. Their place is therefore both limited and temporary. Love alone points to perfection and totality; and compared with this, other things are left behind like the ways and achievements of childhood. Paul is suggesting that the Corinthians' preoccupation with spiritual gifts rather than love is a sign of childishness and immaturity. To see that love is the supreme need, and to practise it, is to have attained true manhood and womanhood in Christ. Moreover, the character of Christ enables us to give content and definition to the word 'love' in a day when it desperately needs such definition.

20 : The Example of Christ

1 Peter 2.18–25

Peter's theme from 2.13—3.7 is submission; believers are to submit to secular power (2.13–17); servants to masters (2.18–21a); wives to husbands (3.1–7). Here he pauses to consider the example in submission that Christ has set His people. Submission is not optional for the believer, it is a calling (21a), and the basis of this calling is that Christ also suffered for us, leaving us an example that we should follow in His steps. Two things can be said about Christ's example of submission.

28

The first is that His submission was well pleasing to God, This is implied in v. 20, and is also evident in the fact that in His submission Christ was fulfilling the role of God's suffering Servant in the Old Testament prophecies of the Messiah. It was appointed for Him by God. The second is that His acts and attitudes of submission were redemptive. They had an end in view. He was crucified in weakness, and the weakness of God proved stronger than men, and powerfully effected salvation. This has significant application to those who follow His example, as we shall see. It is important first, however, to note that in describing our Lord's life and ministry in vs. 22 f., Peter quotes extensively from Isa. 53, a prophecy which pre-eminently unfolds the mystery of His atoning sufferings. We could hardly find a more striking evidence that the New Testament writers invariably linked Christ's life and death as belonging together in the atoning work He accomplished for our salvation. His submission in life and His submission in death cannot ultimately be separated.

His submission was redemptive; and about the worth and effect of that redemption two things are said: the first is that the death of Christ introduces a death into our experience which slays our 'old man' and imparts new life. This is healing indeed (24)! The second is that it brings us back to the Shepherd and Guardian of our souls (25), that is, we are brought back into fellowship with God, and into our true destiny.

Finally, if His submission was redemptive in its effects, and suffering is part of our calling because it was first part of His, then, although the cross stands alone as God's finished work for the salvation of men, our suffering submission and love must in some way be redemptive too. It will 'reflect', even 're-enact', His in the world, and so be a means of blessing to others. See 2 Cor. 4.10 ff.

21 : Our Great High Priest

Hebrews 4.14–5.10

The thought in this passage follows directly on that in Heb. 2.1–18, which unfolds the nature of Christ's priestly work, Here it is the character of our great high priest that is presented as the source and inspiration of steadfast living for the believer (4.14, 16). It is the gentleness, understanding, compassion and sympathy of Christ that the writer underlines in His high-priestly character, and we can be sure of these qualities in Him, because He has stood in with us in all our need and tasted the suffering that is the common lot of men (2.18; 4.15; 5.8 f.). The words 'deal gently' in 5.2 ('have compassion', AV) translate a verb which almost suggests 'to stand in the middle of the human situation'. This means not only that a true high priest gets alongside men in their needs and is one with them in all their cares and anxieties, but also that he is able to 'strike a happy mean' in his dealing with their sins, that is, he is neither too hard, nor too lenient, in his treatment of offenders. Neither the critical and censorious nor the soft and sentimental can help us; our need is for one who will not spare us and may whip us soundly, but whose heart will be full of tenderness towards us. Christ fulfils perfectly this 'happy mean', and those most Christlike in His service approximate most closely to His example.

Referring in 5.7–10 to our Lord's fellow-feeling with us, the writer turns our thoughts to the agony of Gethsemane, as if to say 'This is how human He is'. But in what sense can it be said that He 'was heard for His godly fear'? This cannot refer to His prayer, 'Let this cup pass from me', for He drank that cup. It seems to speak rather of His (unrecorded) cries for strength to enable Him to walk the appointed way of the cross. This is the prayer that was heard (Luke 22.43). In v. 8, the phrase 'He learned obedience' does not mean that Jesus learned to obey through His suffering, but rather that He learned what obedience to the Father's will costs. It was thus that He was made perfect (v. 9), in the sense of being brought into His full destiny—'into His own'—as the Redeemer of God's people and author of eternal salvation.

Questions and themes for study and discussion on Studies 17-21

1. What light do the writer's words in Heb. 2.18 and 4.15 shed on the Temptation story in Luke 4?

2. Before Calvary the disciples shrank from the 'cross' principle: after Pentecost they gloried in it. What changed their attitude?

3. In 1 Cor. 13 Paul's picture of the life of love is based on the character of Christ. What does this fact teach us about the nature of the Christian life?

4. How far does Peter's teaching in 1 Pet. 2.11–18 reflect our Lord's in Mark 10.35–45?

5. How does Christ fulfil His high priestly role according to the writer of the Hebrews?

FOUR

His Exaltation (1)

22 : The Shepherd-King
John 2.13–22; 10.14–21

The common factor in these two passages is our Lord's reference to His dying and rising again, and they present Him in two different, though complementary, aspects. In the Temple-cleansing incident His strength and power are revealed, while in the second it is His tenderness as the Good Shepherd that predominates. Both are significant in relation to the death He died. On the one hand, in acting with authority in the Temple at the outset of His ministry He was inaugurating His work by a claim to be the King of Israel and Lord of the Temple. It was a deliberate assumption of the role of Messiah, in terms of the prophecy in Mal. 3.1 ff. And when the Jews asked Him for a sign to justify His actions, Jesus announced that His death and resurrection would authenticate His every claim and action. To speak of His death in this way was to make it plain that it was not something that happened to Him—as tragedy can happen to men—but something that He accomplished and in which He held the initiative. This is made very clear in 10.18 where He speaks of laying down His life of His own accord and taking it again. It is the voluntary nature of His dying that makes His death of unique significance and gives it its infinite worth as an act of atonement and redemption. He is the one man in all the universe on whom death had no claim as of right; that He chose freely to enter death for our sakes makes it a demonstration—and a release—of kingly power for our salvation. He did not simply suffer death, He entered it as a conqueror.

On the other hand, His claim to be the Good Shepherd (10.14) implies that the power in His death is the power of suffering love. The word 'good' in the Greek literally means 'beautiful', and it is the attractiveness of the goodness that is emphasized. 'I, when I am lifted up from the earth,' said Jesus, 'will draw all men to myself' (John 12.32). There is something irresistibly attractive about the dying Saviour. In a way we can never fully understand, when Christ crucified is proclaimed, He draws men to Himself, and this is how they heed His voice (10.16).

23 : Weighed—and Found Wanting

Mark 12.1-12; Acts 4.5-12

The connecting link between these two passages is not only the quotation that both use from Psa. 118 about the stone the builders rejected, but also the theme of the rejection of the gospel. The parable of the vineyard sums up the whole history of the Jews. The vineyard represents the Kingdom of God. To the Jews, here represented by the husbandmen, was given the privilege of bringing in the Kingdom. But all along they failed, and their failure ultimately involved the forfeiture of all their privileges and advantages, and the transfer of them to others. The whole of Old Testament history is therefore covered by the parable. The servants in the parable represent the prophets from Samuel to John; one and all, their ministry was rejected. Jesus, then, simply rehearses the facts of history before His hearers, and in the latter part of the parable reveals what is about to happen—a dramatic situation and a devastating experience for His hearers who perceived that He was describing them. Most wonderful of all, however—and this is the force of the quotation from Psa. 118—God has so manifested His sovereignty as to accomplish from this rejection and rebellion of His people, and their dastardly hatred of His Son, a glorious redemption for the whole world. As Paul puts it in Rom. 11.15, God's rejection of the Jews means the reconciliation of the world.

The full content and significance of this idea is given in Acts 4.5-12. Here, the prophecy in the parable has become

33

historical fact, the tenants of the vineyard have put the owner's son to death, and the vineyard is about to be given to others. The rejection now, however, is seen to be less excusable than ever, for by asking 'By what power or by what name did you do this?' they were rejecting what Peter had already said in 3.16 by way of explanation, and demanding another. But there is no other explanation than that it was in the Christ whom they had slain, and whom God had raised up, an incalculable power for good had been let loose on the world. The stone that the builders rejected had indeed become the head of the corner, and the only source of salvation for all who believe in Him.

24 : 'Seeing and Believing'

John 20.1–18

One of the important lessons in John's account of the resurrection lies in his description of how its significance dawned on the disciples who went to the tomb. The word 'see' occurs repeatedly in the passage—vs. 1, 5, 6, 8, 12, 14, but the Greek is not the same in each case. Three words are used, each with a different shade of meaning. When Mary came (1) she saw that the stone was removed; this word describes the physical act of seeing. She noticed the fact, as John also did (5) when he saw the linen cloths lying. When Peter, however, saw them, another word is used, suggesting that his attention was arrested by what he saw. It was unusual, and made him look again. This word is also used in v. 12 when Mary saw the two angels. It registered with her as something unusual. Yet another word is used in v. 8 of John's 'seeing', describing an experience, and denoting perception, knowledge, understanding, and spiritual illumination. He saw, everything became clear, and he believed. What he saw was the significance of the resurrection, for it dawned on him that the claims Jesus had made about Himself, hitherto only partly comprehended, were the simple truth. He was God manifest in the flesh, as He had said, and He had passed through death as its Victor and was now alive for evermore.

This kind of 'seeing' is also evident in the encounter Mary had with the risen Lord in the garden. Mary did not come to faith and enter into peace through seeing the risen Lord with the eyes of the flesh; indeed, the physical act of seeing Him produced no reaction in her at all, for she did not even recognize Him. It was the inward 'seeing' which followed (16) that made the difference, a 'seeing' comparable to that of John's in v. 8. The words which follow in v. 17 confirm that the new relationship with Him was not to be the same as before, dependent on touch and sight—but on something more important, namely faith. What John expresses in v. 31 as the purpose of writing his Gospel had first of all become true of himself and his companions. They had 'seen' and believed. What do you see in this story?

25 : 'He Ascended into Heaven'

Acts 1.1–14

Two points in particular call for attention in this passage. The first concerns the significance of the forty days (3) during which Jesus showed Himself to His disciples. The reason why He did not ascend to the Father's right hand immediately after His resurrection is twofold: firstly, He had to open the disciples' understanding to the meaning of the work He had accomplished in His death and resurrection; and secondly, He gradually taught them, by appearing and disappearing among them, to realize that His presence with them did not depend on their seeing Him. They were being taught to believe He was with them, independently of anything they might see, hear, or feel. This was an indispensable preliminary to their reception of the Spirit (4, 8).

The second point is the ascension of Christ. Concerning this two things must be said. Its first significance is that He 'entered into heaven itself, now to appear in the presence of God on our behalf' (Heb. 9.24), to present the merits of His atoning work before the throne of God. In this He fulfils the office of the high priest in the Old Testament economy, whose function was to offer sacrifices for the people, to intercede

35

for them, and to bless them from God. But it was also His enthronement and exaltation, His receiving of the Name that is above every name (Phil. 2.9), His coronation as the mighty Victor. The Christ whom we worship is not only our High Priest but a glorious King, to whom all power is given in heaven and in earth. We must not, however, think of Christ's ascension as something separate from the rest of the gospel, but as the triumphant culmination of the tremendous 'movement' of eternity which is the goodness of God to man. It is the incarnation, life, death, resurrection and ascension that constitute the saving work of Christ—and never one without the others. But it is the ascension as the climax of His finished work that is the basis of the ingathering of souls that was to take place. He won the right to men's allegiance by His death and resurrection, and the great capitulation was about to begin, at Pentecost.

26 : The Death of Death and the Death of Christ

Acts 2.22–36

The decisive importance of this passage is that it shows unmistakably what is the true nature of the gospel. Peter asserts that the fulfilment of Joel's prophecy (17–21) is associated with the life, death, resurrection and exaltation of Jesus—that is, that the outpouring was associated with the coming of the Messiah of the prophetic Scriptures, and that the Jesus whom he now proclaimed was that Messiah. There is no thought here of Jesus being merely a great religious leader martyred for his ideals. True, Peter presses the charge of the crucifixion on the Jews, but says that behind this lay the definite plan and foreknowledge of God. Christ's death was 'according to plan', the divine plan of redemption foretold in the prophetic Scriptures. It is this apostolic interpretation of the historical facts that constitutes the gospel. And it is interpretation according to the Scriptures—this is the point of the quotations from the Old Testament in vs. 25–28 and vs. 34 f., for they show that everything held together and was rooted in the divine revelation and purpose from the beginning.

36

The significance of v. 24 is considerable—death could not hold Jesus—for it indicates that we are to view the gospel as the divine counter-strategy over against the inroads death had made in the life of man. What Peter is saying is that when death spread to all men (Rom. 5.12) the living God declared that death should not have the last word in the human situation. The gospel is God's intervention for man's sake, to make war on death, and destroy it. In the fullness of time He came, incarnate as man, to do battle as man, for man, against the bitter enemy that reigned over all mankind. And He, who did not need to die, chose to die, thus making Him a deadly and invincible foe for the king of terrors, for He carried the war into the enemy's stronghold, taking death by storm and destroying it from the inside. And His resurrection is the practical proof that this was no fiction, but a glorious fact, which His exaltation and the subsequent coming of the Spirit brought home to the glad experience of the apostle band that day. This glorious triumph was accomplished for us too!

27 : The Apostolic Gospel and its Reception

Acts 13.16–43

Here is a characteristic example of apostolic preaching. As always, the emphasis is on the fulfilment of Old Testament prophecy in the life, death and resurrection of Christ. Paul begins with the law and the prophets that had just been read in the synagogue (15), and sweeps through Old Testament history, showing its inner meaning, and its fulfilment in the good news of the gospel. The faith of the fathers, he means, was faith in the promise of redemption, and what they all looked forward to has now taken place in the coming of Christ. Paul stresses the immense privilege given to his own generation to be the witnesses of His coming (26). True, those to whom He was sent neither recognized Him nor understood the prophecies concerning Him (27), and demanded His death. But God overruled this, for what they did was sovereignly used by God to accomplish salvation for mankind, fulfilling the promise made to the fathers by raising Jesus from the dead (33).

The substance of this good news, and the meaning of the promise, is revealed in v. 38 as the forgiveness of sins and justification. It was to procure this that Jesus died and rose again. In v. 39, 'freed' translates the Greek word for 'justified', and Paul's reference in what follows to the law of Moses points the way to a true understanding of the Old Testament. The Jews' misunderstanding lay in supposing that justification could come by the law, whereas it is clear both from the New Testament and from a proper insight into the Old, that the law was never meant by God to be a means of salvation. Its purpose was preparatory; it was 'our custodian until Christ came, that we might be justified by faith' (Gal. 3.24), fulfilling its function by convincing us of sin (Rom. 3.20) and therefore of our need of Him.

One wonders whether Paul felt it specially necessary to utter the word of warning in vs. 40 f. Perhaps he saw then what he was so often to see afterwards; restlessness and resistance on the part of the Jews, and refusal of his message. At all events, it is always proper for such a warning to be given, since it is a very critical—and may be a fatal—thing to react wrongly to the word of grace.

Questions and themes for study and discussion on Studies 22-27

1. What did Jesus refer to in the words 'My hour has not yet come' (John 2.4)?

2. The passage from Psa. 118 quoted in Mark 12.10 and Acts 4.11 is also quoted in 1 Pet. 2.7. What further insight does this third reference give?

3. How far would it be true to say that the full significance of the resurrection of Jesus dawned on the disciples only at Pentecost?

4. What is the relationship between the ascension of Jesus and the gift of the Holy Spirit?

5. How does Peter's message in Acts 2.22–36 compare with those in Acts 10.34–43 and Acts 13.17–41?

6. How far could it be said that Paul's words in Acts 13.26 ff. are the seed-plot of his later teaching in the Epistle to the Romans?

38

FIVE

His Exaltation (2)

28 : 'According to the Scriptures'
1 Corinthians 15.1–11

This chapter is one of the most magnificent in all Scripture. Its first section (1–11) deals with the fact of the resurrection, and what follows with its implications. Paul sets his teaching in the context of the gospel message itself (1), reminding us that we are not entitled to emphasize the death of Christ to the exclusion of the resurrection, or vice versa. Both are essential. The message he delivered at Corinth was 'that Christ died for our sins . . . and that He rose again the third day according to the scriptures' (3 f.); this is what constitutes the gospel.

We are given in these verses a threefold proof of the reality of the resurrection of Christ. First, the existence of saved men and women (1 f.)—the fact of the Church—is a compelling proof of the resurrection, for here are men and women who themselves have been raised to newness of life. Note Paul's words, 'you received . . . you stand . ; . you are saved'. This is what lifts the doctrine out of the realm of theory and speculation, and makes a believer certain. He knows—for it has happened to him.

Secondly, Paul substantiates the resurrection from the Scriptures (4). The resurrection of Jesus was not a hastily concocted fiction stuck on to the story by the disciples to give it a happy ending, but something integral to the strategy of God and foretold by the very Scriptures that prophesied His death (cf. Pss. 2.7; 16.10; 22.22 ff.; Isa. 53.10).

Thirdly, there is the testimony of the eyewitnesses (5–8).

39

The implications here are very impressive and far reaching, particularly the fact that most of the five hundred referred to in v. 6 were still alive and could have disputed Paul's assertion if it had not happened. When one thinks of the flimsy evidence on which scientists sometimes make such confident pronouncements, and how prone some are to dispute that on which the gospel is based, it becomes only too clear that their objections to the Christian message are often based on moral, rather than intellectual, grounds. Once the validity of the evidence given here is admitted—and it is far too authentically documented to be questioned—one is obliged to kneel down and own Christ Lord of all. And this is what the proud heart of man is not prepared to do.

29 : 'Christ is Risen'

1 Corinthians 15.12–28

In these verses Paul deals with the implications of the resurrection. Some in Corinth held that there was no resurrection from the dead, i.e. that resurrection, as a concept, was unthinkable. Paul here shows the logical conclusion of this Sadducean unbelief. If resurrection *per se* is unthinkable, Christ could not have risen; and if Christ is not risen, 'your faith is futile, and you are still in your sins' (17). The explanation of this categorical statement is that the resurrection of Christ was God's imprimatur on the finished work of the cross, the divine seal of approval on the worth of His atoning death. Christ died for our sins, suffering as the Just for the unjust, to bring us to God, being set forth as a propitiation, making atonement for sin—all this the Scriptures teach, and to this He bore witness when He cried 'It is finished.' But was He right, and are these statements true? How can we be sure? What proof is there that atonement *was* made? Ultimately, only God could answer these questions, and the resurrection was God's 'Yes' to them all, His proclamation to the world that the death of Christ was sufficient to procure our everlasting salvation. This is how central the resurrection of Christ is. It alone enables us to proclaim with assurance that 'Christ died for our sins.'

Next, Paul links the resurrection of men with that of Christ (22 ff). Adam and Christ are spoken of as representative figures, the heads of the old humanity and the new. When Adam sinned, all the family of men sinned and fell in him. But there is a second family, the family of God in Christ, all members of which partake of the blessings of its Head. All that Christ did was for us, and when He triumphed over sin and Satan, we became victorious in Him. Thus, those who believe in Him not only share in His risen life now, but shall do ultimately in the fullest measure (22, f.). The redeemed in Christ shall finally be gathered home, and the resurrection of Christ as first-fruits is the pledge and guarantee of the final harvest when the Church is glorified. Ultimately, all in the universe will be subdued under Him (25–28). The resurrection of Christ has incalculable, even cosmic, repercussions.

30 : Head Over All Things—For Us!

Ephesians 1.15–23

Paul now passes from his exposition of our riches in Christ (3–14) to the prayer that we might enter fully into them. It is a prayer that the Holy Spirit will make personal in us the work of Christ for us. It has three parts, corresponding to statements made in vs. 3–14, the first with v. 4, the second with v. 11, the third with v. 13.

The hope to which He has called us is the hope of glory (Col. 1.27), of our ultimate conformity to His image (Rom. 8.29; Phil. 3.21). When once the grandeur and magnitude of this reality grips us, it will become an anchor of the soul (Heb. 6.19), making us steadfast and immovable in all the storms of life. In the New Testament 'the blessed hope' is an incentive and encouragement to holiness and steadfastness of life.

The phrase 'in the saints' (18) can mean 'among the saints'. Paul would then mean it is not possible fully to know the riches of God's glorious inheritance except in fellowship. It is when we are together that that fullness dawns on us. If we take 'in the saints' literally, it refers to what God is intent on doing in us for Himself, in preparing a people for His own possession (cf. Eph. 5.27). To know what God is aiming at in our lives will not only help us understand all His dealings with us, but also enable us to co-operate gladly with Him in willing obedience and submission.

This passage owes its place in this series on Christ's person to Paul's third petition. Here (19 ff.) two points must be noted. One is that the 'power in us who believe' is the Holy Spirit, since it is the same power as was at work in Christ, who offered Himself without blemish to God through the eternal Spirit (Heb. 9.14), and was designated Son of God with power according to the Spirit of holiness by His resurrection from the dead (Rom. 1.4). The other is that the Spirit comes to us to work the same pattern in us as He did in Christ, 'repeating' in us the process of death, resurrection, and exaltation. His being made head over all things was not for Himself alone, but for us (22), and He 'makes over' that immense victory to us by His Spirit. It is for a knowledge and understanding of this that Paul prays so earnestly in these verses.

31 : Stooping to Conquer

Philippians 2.1–13

This passage contains one of the mightiest and most sublime utterances Paul ever made. It describes the mind of Christ as He became incarnate to save us. Paul's portrayal of the downward steps of Christ's humiliation is very moving. From glory to shame, from crown to curse He came, to stand with us in our woe and lift us from it by the infinite worth and power of His descent. 'In the form of God' means that constitutionally, in the essence of His being, He was God. Yet He did not count equality with God a thing to be grasped, to be hugged to Himself, but voluntarily surrendered it in the interests of the world's redemption. A contrast between the first and last Adam may lie behind Paul's thinking here. In the story of the Fall (Gen. 3) it was precisely equality with

42

God that Adam did grasp at ('you will be like God'). But Christ, who could have claimed this as of right, regarded it as something to be surrendered. Not in that way was He to attain man's submission to Him as Lord. So He emptied Himself, not divesting Himself of His Godhead or of the attributes of Deity, as some would have us believe, but pouring out His soul to death (Isa. 53.12), accepting death as obedience to the Father's will. Because of this God highly exalted Him—this is the point of 'therefore' in v. 9. The humiliation is the basis of the exaltation. The significance of this is profound and decisive: Christ's exaltation to the Father's right hand and His being given a name mean that He was raised to a place of equality with God. What He refused to grasp as His right is now freely given Him by God as the fruit of His passion and victory. The 'name' He is given is that of Yahweh, Lord. Paul is clearly quoting from Isa. 45.23 and attributing to Christ what originally belonged to Yahweh.

The summons 'work out your own salvation' (12) corresponds to 'Have this mind among yourselves' (5). When that awesome self-emptying and subsequent exaltation (6–11) touches our lives, as it does by the operation of the Spirit of God, it will produce in us the kind of spirit Paul describes in vs. 1–4, and the mind of Christ will be manifest in us.

32 : Suffering and Glory

1 Peter 1.10–21

The distinctive importance of this passage is that it relates the sufferings and subsequent glory of Christ to the Old Testament prophecies. The gospel has its roots in the Old Testament, and there is an essential unity between the Old and the New. The whole of the biblical revelation has to do with the gospel, and this fact is an indispensable key to a proper understanding of the Scriptures as 'the history of the promise'. This enables Peter to speak of the Spirit of Christ at work in the prophets (11) without any sense of incongruity. The Christian position commits us to this viewpoint, for the doctrine of the Trinity implies the *eternal* Sonship of Christ, and it is the Spirit's work to testify of Him, in whatever age (John 15.26). In the old dispensation the vision was for an appointed time; their hope was in the promise, and in the God-appointed symbols and shadows of things to come, which pointed beyond themselves (12). Hence the reference to Christ as 'a lamb without blemish or spot' (19): the sacrifices were shadows cast on the course of history by the Lamb slain from the foundation of the world. He is the truth of all the sacrifices, and the relation between the two great dispensations is that of promise to fulfilment. It was this that the Spirit revealed to the prophets.

The sufferings and glory of Christ are reflected in the two-fold strand in the Old Testament's prophetic teaching, some prophecies stressing the idea of the coming of a glorious King, others depicting the suffering Servant of God. This second idea was largely obscured and misunderstood by the Jews, hence the difficulty the disciples had with the thought that 'the Son of man must suffer' (Mark 8.31), and the apostolic insistence, later, that this was the heart of the gospel (Acts 17.3). This was the good news they preached through the Holy Spirit sent from heaven (12).

'Ransomed' (AV, 'redeemed', 18) has the force of 'set free by the payment of a price', and Peter speaks here of the great deliverance from sin's guilt and power achieved by the blood of the cross, which establishes the new covenant that ends the old dispensation and fulfils it. Christ is the Passover Lamb by which men are brought into a new relationship and fellowship with God.

33 : The Magnitude of Christ

Revelation 1.9–20

John is on Patmos, in exile for Christ's sake, but he is conscious of belonging to two worlds: he is also 'in the Spirit', and this unseen world becomes more vital and real than his visible experience of exile as the living, exalted Christ (17 f.) breaks in on his consciousness, imparting in vision a message of wonderful encouragement to hard-pressed believers in every age.

Three points in particular should be noted. The first is the assurance that no matter how severe the suffering and pressure experienced by God's people may be, the living Christ stands among them. Independent of any consciousness or sense of His presence and even in the teeth of the most realistic impressions that deny it, He is there. His Alpha and Omega (the first and last letters of the Greek alphabet) indicate that tribulation is bounded by the living Christ. He is there before it begins and after it is over. Every Patmos is encompassed by the everlasting arms.

The second point is the impression of great magnitude conveyed in the words that describe the Christ who appeared to John, eyes like a flame of fire and voice as the sound of many waters. Above all else this is the conception of Christ that the Church needs in time of trial. What John needed, surrounded as he was by the barren rocks of Patmos and the cruel jailors, with the wide sea cutting him off from fellowship with God's people, was the sight of majesty and glory, and this is what was given him in the vision of the exalted Christ in the midst of the lampstands.

Finally, something needs to be said about the nature of Christ's exaltation. It is not merely a sequel to His dying and rising again, or the culmination of His saving work. It is that; but it is more, for that saving work was a triumph over all His enemies. His exaltation is therefore His assumption of the place of power where He takes action to fulfil His plans for His Church. This is an 'official' position, which gives Him authority over all, and is what having 'the keys of Death and Hades' means. He is in sovereign control. Well might He say to John, 'Fear not'! Who could fear with such a glorious Lord standing with him?

Questions and themes for study and discussion on Studies 28-33

1. What can we learn from 1 Cor. 15. 1–11 about the preaching of the early Church?
2. What is it about Christ's resurrection (1 Cor. 15.12–28) that is so crucial for the very existence of the Christian faith?

3. What is the relevance of Christ's exaltation to His Church today?
4. What does Phil. 2.5–13 tell us about what God thinks of His Son's self-emptying?
5. If the gospel that centres in Christ is rooted in the Old Testament Scriptures (1 Pet. 1.10 ff.), how is it that the Jews were so blind to its truth?
6. On what grounds can we legitimately apply to ourselves the assurances that were given to John in the vision that came to him on Patmos (Rev. 1)?

SIX

His Return (1)

34 : Before the End

Matthew 24.1–14

The apostolic certainty of the return of Christ was rooted in the teaching of our Lord Himself on this subject. In this great chapter, His teaching on the Last Things emerges from the disciples' twofold question in v. 3 about the destruction of the Temple (2) and His coming. It seems clear that these events were closely associated in their thinking, but our Lord's reply does not imply acceptance of a close temporal connection between them. Two perspectives are in view in His teaching, and this complicates interpretation. Although some of His statements clearly refer to the fall of Jerusalem and others just as clearly to the end of the age, some could apply to either.

In vs. 4–14 Jesus speaks of general matters, principles almost, applying equally to A.D. 70 and to the End. He says in effect: 'These are to be the general characteristics of the age; in greater or lesser degree this is how things will be in the world until I come again.' So many of them reveal the instability of this present order, affected as it is by sin, and reveal the necessity for the coming of God's order, the only really stable one, which is to be ushered in by the return of Christ. He instances in particular three facts: imposters in religion (5, 11), wars and rumours of wars (6 f.), affliction and persecution (9 f.). He exhorts, however, against discouragement (6), for these are the circumstances in which the gospel will be preached in every age. There are no ideal conditions in which to work for Christ; there will always be

47

opposition. But the gospel will be preached (14). This is the one message that can bring the stability of the new order into human life as it is lived in the old world, for, as Paul reminds us, 'if any one is in Christ, he is a new creation; the old has passed away, behold, the new has come' (2 Cor. 5.17). Patient endurance will result in final salvation. Here then our Lord's realistic teaching makes us aware of the fact that, until His return, we live in an evil world, but we do so with a great hope in Christ burning in our hearts.

35 : Tribulation and the Son of Man's Return

Matthew 24.15–28

The great eschatological discourse of our Lord continues. All the troubles and trials of which the earlier verses speak find their climax in the teaching of these verses. A time of great tribulation is described, and this is indicative of the kind of conditions to be expected throughout the course of the age. Everything here is applicable to A.D. 70, and took place then. Although this is true, some of the language at least suggests a further and deeper fulfilment at the approaching end-time. In our study of Isa. 7.1–17 (Study No. 9), we saw another example of the principle of double fulfilment. The emphasis on tribulation in v. 21 indicates that in this time of crisis the pressure (for that is the literal meaning of the word translated 'tribulation' there) that is a constant factor in every age will be greatly intensified.

Something more then than the fall of Jerusalem is in view, viz. nothing less than the great climax of evil prior to Christ's coming. This means that what might otherwise have filled the hearts of God's people with fear itself contains a message of hope, for beyond the tribulation lies the coming. The application to more than one event is confirmed by the reference to Daniel (15), for this prophecy was certainly fulfilled in 168 B.C. when Antiochus Epiphanes, the Seleucid ruler of Syria who claimed authority over the Jews in Palestine, erected an image of Zeus in the Temple. Christ's use of the language of Daniel to describe something yet to happen gives it a multiple meaning, for if it had a more immediate fulfilment in 168 B.C., and a later one in A.D 70, why should it be thought unlikely that yet another fulfilment should lie in the future, at the end? This means that every onslaught of persecution, every time of trial and difficulty for the Church, has been used by her Lord to make her ask, 'Is He coming soon?'. Such experiences, difficult as they may be, are good for us if they make us live not only in the light of the Christ who has come, but of that same Christ's return.

36 : The Signs of His Coming

Matthew 24.29-44

This next section of the Olivet prophecy certainly looks beyond the fall of Jerusalem to the coming of Christ. Three points specially should be noted. First (29-31), the terms describing Christ's coming—clouds of heaven, power and great glory, the trumpet call, the gathering of the elect— correspond to 1 Cor. 15.51 ff.; 1 Thess. 4.15 ff.; Rev. 10.7, and consistency of interpretation demands that we take all these passages as referring to the same things. Comparing Scripture with Scripture is necessary if we are to avoid anarchy of interpretation. The reference to cosmic disturbances associated with the end-time (29) bears witness to the biblical teaching that the sin of man affects the whole creation, and this explains our Lord's language here. In the last days when evil rises to the summit of its arrogance in its defiance of God, the very universe will reel under the impact of the clash.

Secondly, the parable of the fig tree (32-35) may be taken as an ordinary metaphor, meaning that as it is certain that summer will follow when the first leaves are seen on the fig tree, so also the coming of Christ will follow these signs (29). But there may be a deeper meaning, although interpreters are not all agreed on the matter. The fig tree was a symbol of Israel, God's chosen people. Perhaps Jesus is indicating that the Jews are God's signpost in history, and that when things happen with the Jews it is a sign that God is going to act.

In this connection, 'generation' (34) can have the meaning of 'a race or family of people'. It is not without significance that the Jewish people, in spite of repeated attempts to destroy them, have remained in existence because God wills them to do so.

Thirdly, Christ ends with a solemn exhortation in which the attitudes of carelessness and watchfulness are contrasted. The unthinking complacency, indifference and ignorance that characterized the days of Noah (37–39) will be repeated at the end-time. It is a picture of the secularization of society. Over against this, He stresses the necessity of watchfulness in view of the sudden and unannounced nature of His coming (42–44). Here we find the true purpose of prophecy: its challenge is not speculative, but moral. We do not understand it aright unless it makes us watch and pray.

37 : Reckoning Time

Matthew 25.31–46

This picture of the final judgement bases judgement fairly and squarely on works, while faith is not mentioned. This is perplexing and disturbing to many, but there is no suggestion that salvation can be earned by good works; rather faith is presupposed. A true believer is 'created in Christ Jesus for good works' (Eph. 2.10), and where these are lacking, a question mark must be placed over against a man's profession. Good works do not themselves argue that a man is justified before God, but their absence shows he is not. 'Faith without works is dead', 'Faith working through love' —these are the propositions Jesus deals with here. That this is how to interpret the passage is corroborated by the words in v. 34, 'Come, O blessed of my Father, inherit . . .' One does not earn or deserve an inheritance: it is a gift, and comes through standing in a certain relationship to the one who bestows it. Above all, those who do inherit are said to be blessed by the Father. This is how salvation begins, and this fact forbids us to reverse Jesus' words and deduce the possession of salvation from the evidence of good works.

For this would mean that every humanitarian or philanthropic work would argue a Christian testimony, which is far from being the same. Giving a cup of cold water is a kindly act, but it may or may not be a Christian one. It is only Christian if it is done by a Christian.

It is sins of omission, not of commission, that Jesus condemns here. Men are blind and impervious to human need because they are preoccupied with themselves. The reason why we fail to feed the hungry and visit the sick is that so many other things occupy our attention. This is why the primary need is to be blessed by the Father, for the blessing He gives is a cross that slays the self-life and re-creates us new in Christ for self-forgetful service to others. Judgement, then, is on the basis of love. Acts and attitudes of love are what salvation, when real, always produces. The fruit of the Spirit is love, and love is what Christ will look for on the day of judgement. 'Have you loved?' He will ask. We should beware however of misunderstanding what the New Testament means by 'love'. A Christian's works are produced by Christian love, which is not simply love for man but love for Christ's sake and out of love for *God*.

Questions and themes for study and discussion on Studies 34-37

1. In the light of Jesus' words in Matt. 24, how true is it to say that every crisis time in history is a foreshadowing of His coming?

2. What are the main differences between the true Christ and false Christs?

3. How are we to relate the 'signs' of the approaching end in Matt. 24.29 ff. to the emphasis in vs. 36 ff. on the suddenness and unexpectedness of Christ's coming?

4. 'Son of Man', 'King', 'my Father', 'Lord'—what do these expressions tell us about Christ's glory? (read Matt. 25.31–46 in the light of its opening verse).

SEVEN

His Return (2)

38 : 'Sincere and without Offence'
Philippians 1.1–11; 3.17–4.1

Paul speaks here of the return of Christ in relation to the completion of the work of grace in the believer. In giving thanks for the Philippians, he expresses his confidence that the good work of redemption that has been begun in them would continue without remission until the coming of Christ consummated it. The recurring reference to the day of Christ (1.6, 10) shows that Paul's eyes were always upon the return of Christ and that he would have his readers to live also in the light of that great event.

Two things are said about this 'good work'. First, there is a marvellously mysterious interaction of divine sovereignty and human responsibility involved in it, not merely in the sense expressed in the famous words of 2.12 f., but in the sense that Paul himself had responsibility in the matter. 'The ground of my confidence that this good work will continue,' he says, 'is that I hold you in my heart'—i.e. within the divine sovereignty at work in salvation and sanctification there is a place for the prayers of God's people, for He uses it to begin and continue the work of grace in men's souls. The kind of prayer He uses is indicated in vs. 9–11; its true spirit in v. 8, and its fruits in vs. 10 f.

Secondly, in 3.17 ff. the prospect of the day of Christ which will consummate the good works of God is held out as an incentive to holy and steadfast living. The coming Christ is our Saviour. At the cross He secured our salvation. Now He is glorified and not only will our bodies be made like His but this will be done by that almighty power which He wields as the risen Lord and which will secure the complete fulfilment of all the purposes of God through Him. Paul encourages the Philippians to live as he and those who have followed his example live—as citizens of Christ's heavenly kingdom. A day will come when their lowly bodies —marred by sin, yet bearing even now the marks of restoration to the divine image through His good work in them— will be changed and will share to the full the nature and inherent qualities of His glorified body. This is incentive enough to walk the way of the cross (3.7–14), following the apostolic example.

39 : The Comfort of His Coming

1 Thessalonians 4.13–18

Paul wrote these words to correct the Thessalonians' misunderstanding of what he had taught them about the return of Christ during his ministry at Thessalonica. While they awaited His coming some of their number had died, and the question that now worried them was: had they been robbed by death of the Christian hope? Had it passed for ever beyond their grasp because they had died before Christ came to take His people to Himself? Paul's answer is that there will be no difference between those who are alive at Christ's coming and those who have already died, for the coming of Christ will usher in the resurrection of the dead, and those alive will be caught up with them to meet the Lord in the air. There is no cause, then, to sorrow over those now asleep in Him.

Christ's coming is a personal return. There have been attempts to spiritualize it to mean either the coming of the Spirit at Pentecost or the coming of death to the believer. The personal character of His return is taught too plainly and too frequently for such attempts to gain any real plausibility. We should compare these verses with 1 Cor. 15.51 f.; Matt. 24.29-31 and Rev. 10.7 to see that Paul is speaking of the last trumpet at the end of time, which heralds the judgement and the day of God. This necessarily means that the resurrection of believers is part of the general resurrection referred to in John **5**.28 f. and Acts **24**.15 (cf. also Matt. **13**.30, 41 f. 49; Rom. **2**.5–10).

A passage like this makes us realize the central importance of our Lord's return for the whole New Testament presentation of the future and fulfilment of the puiposes of God. Resurrection and consummation both await His coming, and what lies beyond this is still presented in terms of Christ. 'So shall we always be with the Lord.'

40 : 'Like a Thief in the Night'

1 Thessalonians 5.1–11

The opening verses of ch. **5** continue the emphasis of the closing part of ch. **4**—the return of Christ. There, however, Paul had dealt with the Thessalonians' ignorance and with problems arising from misunderstanding, while here he reminds them of the implications of things they know very well (2). To know, as they did, about the conditions which would precede the coming of Christ, and, above all, about its unexpectedness and suddenness, bringing terror to the unprepared, ought to produce in them the fruits of watchfulness (4), sobriety (6) and hope (8). The illustration of the thief is a link with our Lord's own teaching (Matt. **24**.43).

Paul stresses here the absolute contrast between light and darkness, day and night (4 ff.). No sentimentalism should make us blunt the sharp edge of these distinctions. Ultimately there are only two possibilities for men: they belong to Christ or to the devil. Indeed, one of the effects of the day of the Lord will be to expose and confirm such distinctions for ever. Our Lord spoke of Himself as the Light of the World, and it is our attitude to Him which determines whether we are sons of the light or the darkness (John **8**.12).

The apostle refers to those who are not Christ's as asleep (6 f.). The unbeliever sometimes suggests that the Christian lives in an unreal world of fantasy. The very reverse is the case. Christ is the Truth and those alone who know Him are awake to things as they are. Reality comes through waking out of sleep, whether in time or in eternity.

Although ch. **5** may give the impression of dealing with the subject more in terms of an event ('that day') than of a Person, vs. 9 f. make it quite clear (as does 4.13–18, which is continuous with it) that this is not really so. The 'day' is important because it is *His* day₁

41 : Judgement and Vindication

2 Thessalonians 1

2 Thessalonians was written to correct misunderstanding and misinterpretation of 1 Thessalonians. The main theme is the same in both, viz. the return of Christ. This is dealt with here in two different aspects, showing the end result of a well defined and distinct process at work in two classes of men, the unbelieving and the believing.

First, the coming of Christ will mean a judgement of retribution on the ungodly, who are introduced here as the source of the Thessalonians' persecutions and afflictions (4). The fact that the Thessalonians are standing firm argues the unseen presence of the Lord upholding them, and this means two things: He uses the tribulation to bring their faith to perfection; and such a situation, in which evil men oppress the good, calls aloud for judgement, and proclaims its certainty. The universe is built on moral lines, and God must vindicate the righteous and punish the wicked, hence this twofold manifestation of judgement, in which rest comes to God's people and affliction to the evildoers (6 f.). Nor is this arbitrary, but the fruition of a continuing attitude of unbelief. Paul distinguishes between those who 'do not know God' and those who 'do not obey the gospel' (8), i.e. the Gentiles and the Jews (cf. Rom. 1.18–2.1 ff.). The Jews have had the divine revelation, first in the law and later in the preaching of the gospel; therefore they are without excuse. But the Gentiles' ignorance is also culpable, for they refused the light of nature and of conscience that might have led them into the knowledge of God.

Secondly, the 'bright side' of judgement is Christ's coming to be glorified in His saints (10), the final consummation for those who, called of God (11) through the preaching of the gospel (10b), have responded to His word, enabling Him to fulfil all His perfect will in them (11). This is described in

55

both negative and positive terms—rest from affliction (7), and glorification (10, 12). The coming of the all-glorious Christ will be the power that transfigures us, because 'the inner glory of faith will be drawn out to its object, and not only shine forth, but in doing so transform the mortal into the immortal. And the beauty of the glorified saint will be seen to be of the same essential beauty as that of the glorified Saviour' (W. Still).

42 : Christ and Antichrist

2 Thessalonians 2.1–12

The Thessalonians had apparently been disturbed by teaching which claimed that the day of the Lord had already come (2), and Paul writes to safeguard against deception (3 ff.). He points out first that, as he had previously taught them (5), Christ's coming must necessarily be preceded by 'the rebellion' and the appearance of the man of lawlessness (3). What this rebellion is he does not specify, but the context indicates a final, climactic revolt against God headed up in an individual who is the incarnation of evil, the Antichrist. There have been many antichrists in history (1 John 2.18), but Paul has in mind the final manifestation in the last days, and until then Christ will not come again. The Antichrist's coming into the open is, however, the work of God, who thus draws him out in order finally to destroy him. Verse 8 shows us how utterly the Lord Jesus will demonstrate by this act of judgement His supremacy and His power over the Antichrist.

Next, in vs. 6 f., Paul refers to a restraining power at work preventing the full expression of evil. He does not explain what he means, and we are left to speculate. Widely different interpretations have been suggested, such as the Holy Spirit, or the Roman Empire, or some angelic being. It is best to see a reference to the principle of law and order, which Paul envisages as being overthrown in the last time, allowing evil to erupt with frightful consequences for the world.

Thirdly, Paul describes something of these frightful consequences (9–12). The activities of this fiendish incarnation of evil are horrific in their implications. Note the blasphemous

56

counterfeit that Satan's work represents here: the man of sin 'comes' as Christ has His coming; he works by supernatural power, as Christ worked by the power of God; he works miracles as Christ did. This is very alarming, and but for one consideration might lead to despair: those who are deceived and perish do so because they have refused to love the truth. Men are not subject to blind forces of fate; moral issues control human destinies, and it is a wrong attitude to the truth that ultimately leads to total deception, and want of sympathy with it that finally damns them. This is no arbitrary vengeance on God's part (cf. Rom. 1.24–28): He is left with no other option than to leave men to the consequences of their own final choice (11), He does so with tears in His eyes (cf. Luke 19.41–44),

43 : The Lamb's Great Bridal Feast

Revelation 19.6–16

The vision John unfolds here is of the final consummation of history and the victory of Christ. It consists of two images; that of the marriage of the Lamb (7 ff.), and that of the victory of the Warrior-King (11 ff.). The choral praise in vs. 6 ff. answers the voice from the throne in v. 5, and describes the jubilation of heaven at the triumph of righteousness. But the preoccupation is not so much with the overthrow of evil as with the glorious reality of the marriage of the Lamb to His Bride. The imagery of Eastern marriage, with the interval between betrothal and marriage during which the bride prepared herself, is fruitful in spiritual illustration. The fine linen (8) with which she is clothed corresponds to the work of sanctification in the lives of God's people: how they are attired on the marriage day will depend on how they live in the interval between their betrothal to Christ and His coming for them. Suffering for His sake, and the sanctifying effect this has on spiritual life, will enlarge their capacity for grandeur and glory in the world to come, just as a wife who brings to her marriage a sound training in practical godliness and faithful living will immeasurably enrich her married life. Furthermore, marriage is not only an end but a beginning

57

also; it is the end of the longing and the waiting, but it is not the end of the story. It opens out into a richer and fuller experience, with unimagined joys and delights, enchantments, responsibilities and privileges.

This glorious consummation is brought about by Christ's coming in power to judge the world (11 ff.). The portrayal of the Faithful and True, The Word of God, King of kings and Lord of lords, almost beggars description. To see the King in His beauty, to see Him come thus, the joy of the universe—joy to those who have owned Him Lord, terror to those who have refused His gospel—this is ultimate reality, for weal or woe. The only thing that will matter then will be to have been on His side, and to have His smile of recognition and commendation. Even to read of it is benediction enough, but to participate in this great event and experience it, defies description. 'Lo, this is our God; we have waited for Him' (Isa. 25.9).

44 : The Urgency of the Gospel Appeal

Revelation 22.6–21

In this epilogue John insists on the authenticity of the visions (6, 18, 19). They are not a series of predictions by a far-sighted man, but a revelation given from above, an unveiling of the truth about our world and of the certainties of things to come.

The solemn urgency of vs. 10–17 reminds us that the purpose of the prophecy is not speculative, or merely to give a better knowledge of the principles that govern the world, but that we should be challenged to come to grips with the truth of the gospel. It is eternal destinies that are at stake, and how men react here to Christ and His gospel will determine their destiny. Hence the warning in v. 10: at all costs men must hear the message and be given opportunity to respond to it before it is too late (12). This is the force of v. 11, 'Let the evildoer still do evil . . .' What a man becomes in this life he will remain for ever; inevitably, inexorably, by their reaction to the gospel, men are deciding their destiny now. Acts, habits, attitudes—these are the fateful choices by which men determine character and its outcome in the eternal order. By nature we all make the wrong choice and invite against ourselves the law by which act ripens into habit, habit into character and character into destiny. But God is greater than this inevitable process of hardening; He is Alpha and Omega, i.e. sin does not have the last word. He can break into the terrible chain of cause and effect that drags men down, and in Christ invites them to come to One who breaks the power of sin and cleanses from all its defilement (14).

Hence the blessedly sweet invitation in v. 17 to 'Come', given by the Spirit and the Bride. The tugging at the heart, the stirring within us, the sudden awareness of the persuasiveness and power of the message—all this is the Spirit saying 'Come.' The Church adds her persuasion to the Spirit's pleading, praying men on Christ's behalf to be reconciled to God (2 Cor. 5.20).

Finally, the warning against adding to or subtracting from the words of the prophecy (18 f.) is crowned by our Lord's testimony to the imminence of His coming and the Church's glad and eager cry, 'Amen. Come, Lord Jesus!'

Questions and themes for study and discussion on Studies 38-44

1. What is the relation between 'pure and blameless' in Phil. 1.10 and 'like his glorious body' in Phil. 3.21?

2. What have Paul's words in 1 Thess. 4.13 ff. to tell us about the nature and significance of Christ's coming?

3. What points of similarity between Paul's teaching in 2 Thess. 1 and that in 1 Thess. 4.13—5.11 make it clear that he is referring to the same event in both passages?

4. What points of comparison are there between Paul's words in 2 Thess. 2 and our Lord's in Matt. 24?

5. What is the relationship of the two images of the consummation of history John uses in Rev. 19 to others used elsewhere, e.g. 'the holy city Jerusalem' in Rev. 21.10 ff.?

6. In setting the appeal of the gospel in the context of the return of Christ, what does Rev. 22. 6–21 tell us about evangelism?